Oracabessa

Lorna Goodison was born in Jamaica, and has won numerous awards for her writing in both poetry and prose, including the Commonwealth Poetry Prize, the Musgrave Gold Medal from Jamaica, the Henry Russel Award for Exceptional Creative Work from the University of Michigan, and one of Canada's largest literary prizes, the British Columbia National Award for Canadian Non-Fiction for *From Harvey River: A Memoir of My Mother and Her People* (2007). Her work has been included in the major anthologies and collections of contemporary poetry over the past twenty-five years, such as the *Norton Anthology of Modern and Contemporary Poetry*, the *HarperCollins World Reader*, the *Vintage Book of Contemporary World Poetry*, the *Norton Anthology of World Masterpieces*, and *Longman Masters of British Literature*.

Along with her award-winning memoir, she has published three collections of short stories (including *By Love Possessed*, 2011) and nine collections of poetry.

Her work has been translated into many languages, and she has been a central figure at literary festivals throughout the world. Lorna Goodison teaches at the University of Michigan, where she is the Lemuel A. Johnson Professor of English and African and Afroamerican Studies.

Also by Lorna Goodison from Carcanet Press

Guinea Woman: Selected Poems
Goldengrove: New and Selected Poems

Lorna Goodison

Oracabessa

CARCANET

First published in Great Britain in 2013 by
Carcanet Press Limited
Alliance House
Cross Street
Manchester M2 7AQ

www.carcanet.co.uk

A CIP catalogue record for this book is available from the British Library

ISBN 978 1 84777 242 8

The publisher acknowledges financial assistance from Arts Council England

Supported by
ARTS COUNCIL
ENGLAND

Printed and bound in England by SRP Ltd, Exeter

To Derek Walcott,
friend and poet

Contents

To Make Various Sorts of Black

To Make Various Sorts of Black   3
Reporting Back to Queen Isabella   5
You Should Go to Toledo   6
New Sketches of Spain   8
O Africans in the Plazas of Madrid   11
Bookmarks for Eyes   12
O Lisboa   14
Not Sadness   15
La Casa Dos Dourados   17
In a Dream My Mother Says   18
In a Little Spanish Town I Google Father Louis   20
In Days of Sail   21
It Is Sunday in Sevilla   22
Sintra's Glorious Eden, After Lord Byron   25
Postcards to Miles   26
Spinning in the Head   28
Ideas of Home   29

Praise to the Limping Angel

Praise to the Limping Angel   33
Limonade Shimmer of Autumn Air Over Aroma of Roast Corn   35
A Cure   37
A Visit to the East   39
At Lunch in Les Deux Magots   41
Remember Us in Motherland   43

HOPE GARDENS

Hope Gardens	53
Quest	55
Gauguin Girl	56
Our First Christian Martyr	57
My Teacher Lena	59
Reading Through the Wall	61
Bookmobile Days	64
Tagore on the Bookmobile	66
Town Drunk Recites Omar Khayyam	68
Need	69

IN THE BLUE BOARDING HOUSE

In the Blue Boarding House	73
A Small Blues for Lady's Gardenia	79
Dance Card	80
Otis Ode	83
Paul Robeson at Athena's	85
Red T-Shirt	87
The Two Sisters Cave	89
Your Heart	90

BYE BOONOONOONOOS

Bye Boonoonoonoos	93
One in a Long Line	94
Our Blessed Country Lady	95
On Sighting Makak by the Roadside	97

The Bear   99
A New State   101
What Does It Mean   105
Everyday Revelations   106
Morning Ballad   109
A Cleanse Petition   111
Note to Self   112
Charlie Chaplin at Golden Clouds   114
Canto I   116

SOON IT IS GOING TO RAIN MILK

Ruth   125
Hagar's Account   126
Be It Done Unto Me According To Your Word   128
Soon It Is Going To Rain Milk   129
St Michael in Sitka   130
Mr Davis Runs the Voodoo Down   132
Some of My Worst Wounds Again   134
From the Bard's Book of Common Prayer   136
Upsetter   139
About the Kind Who Wrestle With You All Night   141
Some More Things You Do Not Know About Me   142
I am a Love Siren   144

Acknowledgements   148

To Make Various Sorts of Black

To Make Various Sorts of Black

According to *The Craftsman's Handbook*, chapter XXXVII
"Il Libro dell' Arte" by Cennino d'Andrea Cennini

who tells us there are several kinds of black colours.
First, there is a black derived from soft black stone.
It is a fat colour; not hard at heart, a stone unctioned.

Then there is a black that is obtained from vine twigs.
Twigs that choose to abide on the true vine
offering up their bodies at the last to be burned,

then quenched and worked up, they can live again
as twig of the vine black; not a fat, more of a lean
colour, favoured alike by vinedressers and artists.

There is also the black that is scraped from burnt shells.
    Markers of Atlantic's graves.
Black of scorched earth, of torched stones of peach;
    twisted trees that bore strange fruit.

And then there is the black that is the source of light
from a lamp full of oil such as any thoughtful guest
waiting for bride and groom who cometh will have.

A lamp you light and place underneath – not a bushel –
but a good clean everyday dish that is fit for baking.
Now bring the little flame of the lamp up to the under

surface of the earthenware dish (say a distance of two
or three fingers away) and the smoke that emits
from that small flame will struggle up to strike at clay.

Strike till it crowds and collects in a mess or a mass;
now wait, wait a while please, before you sweep this
colour – now sable velvet soot – off onto any old paper

or consign it to shadows, outlines, and backgrounds.
Observe: it does not need to be worked up nor ground;
it is just perfect as it is. Refill the lamp, Cennini says.

As many times as the flame burns low, refill it.

Reporting Back to Queen Isabella

When Don Cristobal returned to a hero's welcome,
his caravels corked with treasures of the New World,
he presented his findings; told of his great adventures
to Queen Isabella, whose speech set the gold standard
for her nation's language. When he came to Xamaica
he described it so: "The fairest isle that eyes ever beheld."
Then he balled up a big sheet of parchment, unclenched,
and let it fall off a flat surface before it landed at her feet.
There we were, massifs, high mountain ranges, expansive
plains, deep valleys, one he'd christened for the Queen
of Spain. Overabundance of wood, over one hundred
rivers, food, and fat pastures for Spanish horses, men,
and cattle; and yes, your majesty, there were some people.

You Should Go to Toledo

I'd stared hard at the tongues of flame
over the heads of the disciples; I felt
a dry heat catch fire in my fontanelle.

"El Grec" the docent in the Prado called
him; a stranger in Spain all his days.
"What is it you like about him?" the one
who came from the dark night inquires.

So I say this:

The way his figures struggle and stretch
till they pass the mandatory seven heads
must be about grasp exceeding reach.

The overturning of my temples,
the slant sideways of seeing that open
as I approach his door-sized canvases.

And his storm-at-sea-all-dolorous blue;
and his bottle-green washing to chartreuse;
and his maroon stains of dried oxblood.

The verdigris undersheen of the black coat,
white lace foaming at the throat and wrist
of a knight with one hand to his chest.

How I cling to the hem of the garment
of La Trinidad's broad-beam angel
who resembles my mother when she was

young, strong, and healthy – body able
to ease the crucified from off the cross.

And he who separated from the shades
and sat at table with us in a late night place
redolent with olive oil and baccalau said:

"Then you should go to Toledo."

New Sketches of Spain

i

This train I board at La Latina
will stop next in Aranjuez
where Rodrigo lived.

As a boy he lost his sight.
A friend became his eyes.
One day he was blessed
with a fine-looking wife.

His duende created major
disturbances in his head;
still he composed
the *Concierto de Aranjuez*
for Spanish guitar

(Did no one tell that to Miles Davis?)

The *Concierto de Aranjuez* is:

Gardens of aromatic camellias
Plaintive exquisite birdsong
Sudden exuberant fountains
A small child's death.

These things I have read.

Train from La Latina
take me to Aranjuez.
I must pay Respect Due
to Rodrigo for myself.

ii

We did not stop in Toledo; I watched it frame
itself through the window of the Madrid train.
I acknowledged El Grec's broad brush plains,
ochre and green the rolling dry brush hills,
the old olive trees, the long light glancing off
storied buildings within which highly skilled
craftsmen still discipline hot steel into swords.
And there were lines of laundry strung across
balconies of brutalist apartment blocks, not far
from the site where St. John of the Cross, all but
immured, suffered his way into song's source.
Praise and thanks canticles out of dark night.
Source wash, wash these words, wash my heart.
"Go forth and exult in your glory!
Hide yourself in it and rejoice."

iii

Tell it to Teresa of Avila
advised the thin priest
to whom you confessed
that in divers times
you'd left your body behind

while your weightless core
sifted up toward the ceiling.

There is no one more able
to understand than Teresa
who at times had to cling
to what was bolted down
to anchor herself from being
hauled up into ether;
taken home before her time.

O Africans in the Plazas of Madrid

O Africans I saw you in the plazas of Madrid
with your ethnic jewellery and bootleg DVDs
set down on flying blankets rigged with strings

you pull when shrill sirens swarm the air.
Pull; and blankets pucker into pouches you fling
over shoulder as you leg it.

O Africans you followed the scent of salt to boats
ferrying you for a fee; or you lodged in the maw
of liners; dark humanity released

into metropoles where you make-believe
you are rejoining Africa's assets; her wealth
droughed away in galleons and caravels

helped to erect cities where you sing mournas,
you flog handbags, bracelets, illegal DVDs
and, fleet of foot, flee from police.

O Africans there are reports of new ships
of the desert; panelled, wheeled
vessels freighted with dark men disgorged

from corked holding cells; swallowed
then as living breathing contraband
ejected again to walk the sand trail of tears

back to from whence they came. O Africans
offical word is: *Estos son sólo rumores.*

Bookmarks for Eyes

Enter the old puppeteer; he creaks the stairs
to the upper room where we sit at late dinner

in an inn where a bronzed plumed bird perches
on top of the cold water tap in the ladies toilet.

Turn the water on; it trills like it's in a birdbath.
That bird should be released over the aqueducts,

perhaps to swell the high chorus of swallows
in the gilded choir loft of the great cathedral.

The old puppeteer comes; he has reduced
his craft to two from three dimensions.

He sells stiff paper figures with black beads
glued on, still damp and bulging as eyes.

Bookmarks, he says, they will keep reading
for you long long after you close your eyes.

So we buy a purple one and pray it will not
stain our sincere tries at clean clear prose.

What do You want from me? All I desired
Was a quiet life grafting poems onto roses
singing slow at home near blue mountains.

What am I searching for outside this known
world, why am I a followfashion Columbus
gone off the map, and here there be dragons.

O Lisboa

St. Vincente, patron Saint of Lisbon, stands
in the Largo das Portas do Sol and cradles
a model boat with mariners and two ravens.

He oversees the harbour from the square
of the sun's gates; he guards Alfama's
steep cobbled streets, his scrolled marble
brocade robes have gone deep off white.

Once a ship docked off the Gambia Coast
and took into its hold, unbeknown to all
aboard, a small stowaway:

a boy barnacle; juvenile remora fastened
on to bark then slipped off ship in Spain.
This boy turned man; crossed into Portugal,
addresses Monica and me as "my mothers."

He sells us bead necklaces he's strung himself.
Amber, and an ink stone so blue it's all but
black, same as his own skin is, in reverse.

He gifts us leather bracelets.

Says, "Thank you, mothers, for talking to me"
says he is going to buy supper for his children
and their mother, she like him is Senegalese.

He becomes furtive when a marked car rounds
the corner, whispers, "Policia." St. Vincente,
tent your stone palm. Shelter the ravens.

Not Sadness

says the youth in the souvenir shop.
In Fado what you hear is tone of longing,
longing to be reunited with the love object.

So all of my songs of late have their start
in Saudade, my songs are blue melancholy
sea chanteys of far-from-home sailors

longing for direction. Please tell me why
and what more do You want of me, Song?

I tattooed Your 99 names with a camel-eye
needle in a ring-a-rose around my navel.

I branded Your seal on the soles of my feet.
Now everywhere I set foot I leave Your logo.

Because of you iniquity workers hate me.
After this how could You just leave?

You swapped spit with me, kneaded me
like clay; now the lame and the can't see

follow me in the streets and insist, insist
like You, I'm licensed to make miracles.

That hour You went from me night fell.
Did you consider the fury I'd encounter

on this pitch road set me to pilgrim?
At a wayside shrine I asked Blessed Mother;

first I touched her feet; her cool plaster sandals
were awash with sprays of red roses.

I asked (you know what I asked) begged
to reach Heartease; pleaded with her to reorient

my heart; set it again on the one path
that springs revival roses like those on her sandals.

                Your song like a slow smile reminds of your face
                  says the One who set me to singing in the first place.

I told Mother of the wild beast attacking my sleep.
Slobbers, it chaws at my peace; asked will I survive

sneak assaults from ventriloquist devils speaking
ill in my head; shape-shifting bad card shufflers

who want what they cannot, must not have.

And she said she saw You lock my soul case
before You turned to leave.
And she saw You sword-swallow the key.
And she said futile; futile their ghastly
done-dead-already burglaries.

La Casa Dos Dourados

The shop of saintly relics you called it;
where she was on display in her painted-on
underwear and the clerk dissembled when
pressed to identify the icon of a black woman

one ruler and a half high, limbs hinged
so she sat upright on a ladder-back chair,
knees together, feet sheathed in ankle boots
straight-laced; sweet-faced, embarrassed

to be seen not properly dressed in a shop
window in the Alfama District; you insist
you need to know who she really is; you wait
till the owner is summoned, his best guess is:

She is Our Lady of Montserrat, Black Madonna.
What could have brought her to this, why
has she stripped off her clothes to expose
her thin white tempera chemise and bloomers?

Our lady's home is on a Barcelona mountain.
Attempts to bring her to the plains failed.
Believers make pilgrimage to her shrine
of miracles, but she's come down to us this day.

You're in the valley of the shadow. The Dark
Lady has come to accompany you through this
place on the path where consolations withdraw.
Do like her; be still; yield up all outer.

In a Dream My Mother Says

In a dream my mother says, buy yourself
a refrigerator, turn your warm down.
Frenemies are taking you for a poppyshow;
dialback to chill mode.

> Dear hatchplotter, plothatcher, springe setter.
> Pitdigger, diggerofpit, whosoever diggeth.
> You think you will be the exception, the only
> one who does not fall into the trap you set
> to trip and catch the innocent. Want to bet?

> Dear carnal-minded: unable to distinguish
> spirit from flesh, what you grab and grasp at,
> that is flesh. This: which blows like the wind
> when and wherever it listeth; this is spirit.

Dear digger of pit, you're claiming I dug first;
except mine was no pit, more a grace space
hollowed with my knee-cup begging for rain
blessing to fall on you who blessed with your
mouth even as you inwardly cursed, plotted,
connived, and planned how to cast down from
excellence; false friend you and your coven
of dirty pot cauldron stirrers are now served.

> Cast, without your say-so, in a recasting of *The Crucible*
> (you know what they did that summer)
> Seasoned adepts of trapset must be forgiven for what
> they do, but must be told, have to be told, not to.

Have mercy on youself for sincere effort
put forth in attempt to recreate the kingdom
down here on earth.

So what if you hosted a generous supper?
So what if they who ate of your labour
now lift callous heels against you?

Rejoice. You are officially in the best possible company.

In a Little Spanish Town I Google Father Louis

Tonight, Father Louis, I summon you up
on my computer screen; I kiss my forefinger

touch to the Apple logo, I press it to the eye
in the centre of your high forehead.

I scroll to your prayer, which begins:
My Lord God I have no idea where I am going.

This written after decades spent journeying
in your hermitage, you said you didn't know

where you were going, could not see the road
ahead. But then you said you did know;

you desired to do what would most please
the Beloved. Right intention would lead

to right path, though when you wrote that
you feared yourself lost in the valley.

In the valley of the shadow, the dark
and dreadful, valley of the shadow of death.

In Days of Sail

In the days of sail, Don Cristobal embarked for Cipangu
and India, give him propers, he was no coward
Genoan and crew in three ramshackle ships.

Imagine setting forth across the vast shoreless ocean
of ambition; not knowing if they'd slip and fall off
the edge of a skywide waterworld.

I too these days share that exact same concern.
I too today feel as if the Blessed Isle I set sail for
is not the one on which I have made landfall.

Like Don Cristobal I could refuse to admit
to being lost; I could just bring it off; call it
what it is not. Heartease. Heartease not.

> Lock pickers of my sleep have hacked into my peace;
> change the old code, lock them out please!

> Stop the war in my head waged by the wretched
> who want me to repay what I did not steal.

Thank you, limping angel; you came at morning;
listing hard on your one compromised and one
good leg. *Obrigada* as they say here.

Travel with me tomorrow to Sevilla; guardian
who will not let the enemy of souls prevail.

It Is Sunday in Sevilla

i

And swallows sing over the mellifluous
voices of the choir who chant mass before
the shining incomparable golden retablo

In this mighty cathedral that first was a mosque.

El Señor, we penitents address the Lord
of Lords, unction our hearts
hardened.

Immaculate Mother of el Señor, we come in need
of Mercy. Mercy on us, Mother of Mercy,
Mother of our Lord of all worlds.

Lord of small birds who pick up our petitions
and relay them way beyond cathedral and mosque.

ii

We vote not to remain after mass to take the tour
of Christopher Columbus's tomb; we'd have
to tarry for two more hours then pay extra.

We who took on our tongues the clean host
but received no red wash of wine;
elect to breakfast at a nearby pasteleria.

We make this decision by the tomb of Diego
son of Christopher who ordered his father's
remains shipped to San Domingo.

Seems Columbus was born Admiral of the Oceansea.

Even after death when his ever questing heart stopped
pumping salt blood in Valladolid,

He was anchors away in his coffin-ship to Santo Domingo.

And when France seized San Domingo
from Spain

his remains went over the bounding main
to Havana, Cuba.

From where the what-left of his mortal self
Was crated as precious cargo to Sevilla.

Dust and ashes Don Cristobal now is
settled upon the shoulders of four kings

in this magnificent cathedral that was
first a splendid mosque raised up by Moors.

By the Puerta del Perdón we pause.
By the door of Pardon ask
to be excused

from sins of deed, word, and thought
that we from time to time to time
most grievously have committed.

Scripted in iron calligraphy
are the names of the One
the Compassionate who is strong
on forgiveness and pardon.

The door of pardon allows
entry to expansive gardens
gold with ripe Seville oranges.

Through the Patio de los Naranjos
Dan and Monica; Ted and me:
proceed in love and friendship.

Sintra's Glorious Eden, After Lord Byron

So I remain here in these ruined gardens
of the Moorish castle because I am afraid
to scale the heights.

I did not ascend with you, love, to the turret
where the cultured intrepid Moors looked out
over Sintra's glorious Eden.

Lord Byron called it so when he stayed
at Lawrence's Hotel, where he never slept
alone, being the hard Lord Byron.

He lauded Sintra's lush beauty.
He ate their meat, imbibed their wine.
He washed his mouth upon the people
(The *dead yard* school of poetry).

Two sphinx-faced cats profile with me
by the dry wall of the Moorish castle.
We tryptich under the torn flag flown

by the Moors; the sun is going down;
night will soon come to our ladies house
of woe, like Byron I do not sleep alone.

Husband, hold me in your arms when you
descend; walk me out of this stone garden.
Name me brave, declare me lovely.

Postcards to Miles

i

Dear Miles, I send you postcards from Córdoba.
Here all the corridas are closed; it is Monday.
Today all bulls look laidback like Ferdinand.
All the bulls, my Taurean son, are settled down
beneath the shade of cork trees, chewing slow,
sleek as leather sofas, they surf the horizon
with far-seeing eyes.

ii

Here is one of El Cordobes, most celebrated
bullfighter to enter a corrida, posterboy of bloodsport.
Hipsters in the sixties hung his image on their walls
and built shrines to him lit by candles stuck in bottles
half-sheathed in straw, drained dry of rough red wine.
I drank my share; but, son, I swear I always cheered
for the determined and courageous bull.

iii

The corridas are closed; yesterday these toreadors
in blinged-out pedal pushers and embellished boleros
contended with the toros; they look like fashion
models, these bullbuckers. We are duppy conquerors.

iv

These four gypsy boys and their dogs
occupy the doorway of this cathedral.
In the plaza there is a demonstration against
40% unemployment. One placard reads:
Si no nos dejan soñar, no los dejaremos dormir.
"If you do not let us dream, we will not let you sleep."
The dogs reek. Two of the boys strum guitars.
One strokes the skin of a hand drum,
the other is out cold on the stone steps.

v

This horse is named Estrelita, from her forehead
a white star blazes, she is the horse of our horse-drawn
carriage and she clip-clops down a glorietta
past a small shrine that houses a saint.
Could be one of these:
A Carries book, pen, and eagle – St. John the Evangelist
B Carries a lamb, dresses in lambskin – St. John the Baptist
C Wears a brown habit, carries the holy child, plus book, cross, and flowers
          – St. Anthony, warrior of the desert
D Standup saint of a stepfather holds in his hand the boy Jesus – St. Joseph

Spinning in the Head

When you cross the narrow
Strait of Gibraltar make your
way to Tangier. There are places
there you will find friends.

"Go no farther, go no farther"
cautions spinning in the head.

Name for spinning in the head:
vertigo; word made famous
by fright master Hitchcock.

But this spinning in the head
only makes you want to buy
a honey-coloured felt fez,

bathe clean and dress yourself
in the liquid pleated robes
of the turners.

And with left hand turned down
to earth, right cupped, head
set to the side, and feet bare,
you will whirl for days

"Do, O do for me, what I cannot do for myself."

Ideas of Home

i

Winter has landed; my boot bucks on a stone
surrounded by snow; I swear, I murmur
Oracabessa. "The rock" is what I call home,
all islanders do, and I'm in blessed Ann Arbor,
mainland, where I found safe harbour under
green sea of trees now becalmed, frosted.
Ideas of Oracabessa propel me forward
down the straits of Packard, past the Jewel
Heart centre where a wild beat poet is ash
urned behind red doors. I stop and pay
respect due him. Then I'm urgent, in need
of touchdown upon ground of my being.
On haste to enter into the land of spices
discoverer within sight of gold fields.

ii

Ideas of home propel me up Parliament
Street; straight past the Jet Fuel café where
machines froth and foam fair-trade coffee
and writers and artists sit in window seats
to divine from flat glass screens, do I dare
go in, sit with them, and drink peach tea?

A girl poet hails a youth with a rhombus
of a red bicycle riding over one shoulder:
"Ah, I see, you are carrying your steed."

An actor of a certain age recognized
from real movies (not straight to DVD)
is fed this line by an older man:
"This street is really changing."
The actor registers sadness to hear this.

I have little knowledge of this city's changes.
But this is what I have come to believe: this
Toronto street at times seems like an El Greco
painting, a humming heavenly highway,
alive with every type of human being
out and about their business; and in late fall
light they appear transported; holyrolled,
at peace, as if they've had their fill of Ontario
corn, and bushels, bushels of ink blue berries.

Praise to the Limping Angel

Praise to the Limping Angel

Girl eats greasy meal in Greenwich Village diner,
deep midwinter; she is on break from cashiering.

Miss lady fears she herself is about to break under
rigor routine of eighteen-hour days; both ways,

three-hour train rides and the consequent thunder
of subway cars rolling along in her long long after

she's peeled up gummy metal steps laddering
up to the loud street; engine resonates deep bass

under every thought, all her talk, under drum
thump of young heart original dub body sounds.

In the greasy spoon Miss slops tomato sauce over
fat knot of soft white noodles: octopus on a plate.

Galpickney craves yard food, hot sun, slurps down
sun yolk beaten into egg cream; pays, leaves.

Late, she takes shortcut across Thirteenth Street.
Twenty-one; our Miss thing swears she's charmed.

Praise to night she begins to profit from friendship
with limping guardian spirit; then she was unsure

who it was, she knows now, seraphs are themselves.
Praise to the one with whom damsel lockstepped

the second she turned down Thirteenth; it imped her
stride to its halting own, as they stepped, a shadow

wicked in a doorway pitched a missile meant to kill
or bring down flat. Hail to that host whose footsteps

young woman stepped in; praise moment; too soon
too late, for weapon went wide before or behind

girlchild is sure of nothing but that it bangaranged
with clang din of old iron, as seraph bound her close

and hipjoined they sackraced toward the sign above
Fifth Avenue cinema between Thirteenth and Twelfth.

Limonade Shimmer of Autumn Air Over Aroma of Roast Corn

Slice a lime quick, Miss, for there is a body at work inside this city
        attempting a blockade; we need to engage
            your limonade to cut and clear.

The well-heeled are fled to Fire Island; there is now a way on wide
        Lexington for Sunday market sellers to slip
            past centuries with small crafts.

To hoist up alpaca sweater bannners, fly pennants of woollen scarfs,
        pitch handbags knockoff; hawk food: red meat stews,
            corn, roast and boil.

O limonade vendor you sing sweet as the young Keats's nightingale,
        or a cling cling, or a finch, golden bird friend
            of Atahualpa Inca.

You know the bean counters collecting toll by the Tappan Zee Bridge
        who keep a red-ink ledger of the looking-
            to-earn-a-bread hordes?

They insist there's no place for the poor always with us; slam them against
        stonewalls; but they always rubber ball
            bounce back and walk

to find other pastures; like this black asphalt marked and cordoned off
        outside Lexington's temples of glass
            as market for margin gatherers.

Flashback Sept 1968 when first I was poet in New York, I beheld a man
spin a round wheel of dough; whirled overhead
it tilted into Ezekiel's.

Man plunged dough into fiery furnace, emerged dough crisp as parchment
scroll he split, bid me eat, sweet it entered
– unlike page masticated

by cantankerous old testament prophets – delicious down into my bowels.
From then on, those who live not by bread alone
acknowledge me as friend long lost

and the angel antidote bids me shower every per diem cent into palms
along Lexington; where I bought a book
from one man,

have not read it yet, just bought it so we would engage in just exchange,
fair trade. I dedicate this to you, purveyor
of limonade as payment

for effective cut and clear service; you sang your stirring limonade song;
you performed removal of obstructions, chanted
how the ones like us have

paid in full and must be guaranteed clear passage through this city's streets;
I too have a song tart and sweet; blessed.
The meek want to hear it.

A Cure

Drum head is pounded as medicine to cure
madness in my Senegalese friend's village.

Diagnosis for dis-ease in the head:
separation from one's life rhythm.

So what a good bush doctor will do is this:
summon the drummers in, arrange them
in a circle around the one who has lost it.

> The drums beat out a range of rhythms
> from console notes coaxed out of female hide
> to baritone rumble of stretched male skin.

The doctor who never sleeps
until a cure is effected
observes the afflicted one.

Notes response to a certain beat.
Doctor urges drummers
concentrate upon beat, repeat

till the patient catches it,
opens mouth, swallows.
Beat enters system;

re-enters blood stream
pumps through veins and arteries
re-sets rhythm gone off at pulse points.

The entire village joins in a dance
with the one who lost but found again
their one and own rhythm.

Hard cases require drumming
for nine straight days and nights,
but all my friend's people have is time.

A Visit to the East

Anita returned from Berlin
              with gloss of that city on her mind so,
                            her voice on the telephone gleams

to say Checkpoint Charlie is now district
for high-end shopping; hard to believe.

Here, Anita: an account of one earlier visit.

It was Boxing Day, nineteen eighty-six
a man   a woman   a young girl   a small boy
crossed over to East Germany from the West.

They were going to see a famous American
cartoonist, a man who found himself divided
on the day they split Berlin city in two.

Sick of being nigger under jim crow shadow,
he'd turned red   was blacklisted   fled
to the Democratic Republic married a comrade

sired one child   a son   a blot on the escutcheon
of the GDR child refused to obey orders
questioned authority; boy was always singing.

The man, the woman, the girl, the small boy
were testing out how a family worked. It did not.
By new year they'd say goodbyes at a taxi stand

and never see each other again.

But that December day they were ushered as a unit
into the apartment of the exiled artist; served tea,
white bread, potted meat sandwiches with butter

cookies they'd carried in a cobalt blue tin as a gift.
The lady communist wife of the artist chain-smoked,
sending up sighs of relief as the four visitors left.

At Alexanderplatz they lined up to eat in the cafeteria,
stood for over an hour to get four seats at the counter
where they could watch chrome on the taps peel off.

On the way back to the station they passed a church;
folk songs soughed through bevelled-glass windows.
The male adult said of the music, "Nothing religious."

On the platform, waiting for the train back to the West,
there was a lean Christmas tree, barely decorated;
one child said: *I thought communists didn't do Christmas.*

At Lunch in Les Deux Magots
for John Edward

Richard Wright and James Baldwin
ate in this very celebrated Paris café
where you and I my dearly beloved

hold these sidewalk seats in the sun
and order salads of spring greens;
tart leaves tonic our wintered mouths.

Here Richard bought a meal for James:
croque madame or croque monsieur
(Gallic cheese toast with ham or without)

Jimmy ate, and later he may even have –
here or elsewhere – sipped absinthe,
one cannot imagine that he did not;

he of the gorgeous frog prince profile
Toulouse-Lautrec would have fixed
on a poster in the age of belle époque.

Wright helped Baldwin to find a room
with room to wield the pen he used
to stab up the reputation of the older man

in an age-old pagan rite that demands
the son is duty bound to slay the father.
One rough business this writing life.

But love; this is Paris in late springtime,
the right season for ripe lovers like us.
Let us drink to the passing of old gods.

Remember Us in Motherland

You say your name is Jacob; your kente cloth shirt
is woven in red and ochre and you wander
the corridors of Angell Hall with a small suitcase

in search of extra texts I give away to students.
I gave them all away but I've retained questions.
Many questions, Jacob, questions and meditations.

The ones transported, do you recall them? Say
sing of them in sorrow songs? hold sacred
their dropped altars and makeshift shrines

the rough heaped tokens left behind by the stolen
as plea for Africa never to forget them,
the ones who dropped blood samples   excrement

hair   teeth   human-seed   fear sweat   rings
necklaces   scab parts of themselves as they departed?

Jacob, might there be griots who in grey headbooks
retain chapters on my own captured foremother
who passed from castle into ship's belly bottom?

My foremother was legend on the Guinea Coast
as the woman who, even with her tongue
pressed down by iron, would not stop chanting.

Jacob, I want to know not for recrimination
for that could make everyone criminal
all over again, I just want to know in the way

of a hard-head poet on whose left knee is a maroon
birthmark triangular: goods, slaves, sugar.
Marked by Africa.

I have a friend who swears fear rode shotgun, sat sour
beside him, protecting him from being surprised by joy,
until the year he made African pilgrimage.

When it was announced they were over the Gold Coast;
fear flew the exit; leapt, kicked the door shut behind
and buried itself in the water casket Atlantic.

Meditation on Another Subject;
About sangomas and soothsayers and mischief:

In Durban, I saw a sangoma on her knees scrubbing
the pavement outside Victoria's market. She locked
eyes with me; she beckoned. I did not go.

There is in me a wild spore. Do you think I'd abandon life
as I know it, plant me in concrete, there to piece and puzzle
the future jigsawed in watergourds?

I've had offers. A Celtic soothsayer sent me tarot cards.
Cellophane on, I passed them to a Jamaican one
who cut them all ways for small profit.

Said I, I'll sight up what I see without aid of marked cards.
My teacher said have no part with witchcraft, malevolent arts,
nor flesh nor spirit mischief.

About mischief, hear my Guinea woman great-grandmother:
"If you beg them, they will beg you." These are true
words spoken to warn us not to borrow from strangers

or spite spirits, currency to buy sweets, or they'll garneshee
your little wages. Me? what I have was earned hard;
ego rubbed to near nub to make room

for not myself and so reduced; athletic imagination can
borrow and Usain Bolt me swift back and forth in time.
I've been propelled to Abena Busia's village.

There I crouched in thickets to see the compassionate
hide the snatched free from coffles; break yoke off
rubbed raw necks, hack chains off linked ankles;

hide captives till mancatchers passed. I leapt from that thicket
of thorns, I could not watch. Jacob, why did some
of your own traffic with soulless demonic human snatchers?

Jacob has no answers; where he is from the subject is never mentioned.

Jacob, what a day it was when they trapped my mother's mother's
mother's mother's mother. All together my foremothers coalesce
into a multiple-breasted goddess; like she around whom a cult

sprung up, her full jugs could stream forth milk; trick, feat
of engineering by temple trickster architect; that said goddess
reigned in ancient temples; her handmaidens blood-let

milk flesh with sharp blades, a remnant exists to this day,
their high priestess Princess Diana; a lovely cutter.
This is not the godesss I want to reference; I call for the return

Of Divine Mother; compassionate guide of collected forebears
carried wide by hot sun, by fertile crescent moonlight; forerunners
represented in a male and female Dogon carving as seen

in a metropolitan museum. All too distracting, Jacob, to keep eyes
flitting from one purloined display to the next; take cleansing
breath; say: Stay eye's eye, stay fixed.

Entire tombs lifted away out of Egypt; such a haul of cool elegant
marbles. Arawak Zemis looking cold, Columbus is gone now,
row them in longboats home.

I spoke so to the golden head of young King Tut; sweetfaced
as my own son. Jacob, I went to Egypt, which too is Africa.
I have journeyed to the north and south of Africa.

On a vernal night in Cairo behind the Al-Hussein Mosque, a downgrow
urchin repeatedly sold us the same crème fraîche garland
of forget-me-nots. Nazira of khol-rimmed eyes sat

on a carved couch; behind her a mirror that had absorbed its image
quota, and brim full, refused to take in even one more; just nacred.
Beneath it sat Nazira. "Why are you crying, you are safe, you

and your Mother, so weep not." So I wept. How does she earn
her bread? Friend Ali said: "She prays, she prays." As we sat there
five customers came and patronized her prayer service.

I was in Egypt. I have pictures to prove it: Me on camelback.
Here I line up my profile with the sphinx. See me poised
at the entrance to a tomb at Cheops but I did not go in.

(dark rooms dark rooms)

Jacob, your voice calls me back. "Where in the world," you ask,
"are the burying grounds for slaves?" And my mind answers:
In the blue boneyard of the Atlantic; along whale roads, railways,

and highways; in mortar edifices of empires, fields of sugar cane,
cotton, tobacco, and humus at the root of cotton trees; in Jazz,
and Rocksteady, in our music. I crossed with my people, you know,

I came with them as chanter girl.

Gladly I toil for my people as chantwelle, to sing of patron saints
of the overworked. Annoint with almond oil the limbs
of girlchildren fanning that wringing wet pile of southern girls

undressed, hoop skirtless Kara Walker belles, *Gone with the Wind*.

Bless the little black girls stirring up soft zephyrs for Miss Scarlett.
Honour, honour to Hattie McDaniel for accepting with dignity
Hollywood's sordid boon.

My son's paternal grandmother was blade thin. She lived in Clarendon
on hard ground out of which she cultivated five bright children;
May her good mother spirit fan harm flies off him.

Can we speak now of Religions? Jacob asks, Like the ones practised
in Haiti and Jamaica? Something they took from Africa to keep them
on the journey, this is what they carried for themselves:
                              Themselves.

Jacob, some say the cords tying us to the Congo are tarred with vengeful
pitch for to tar one's enemies with harm. Can we cleanse that one?
Some say the Yoruba cord conducts news of the future; binds us

double-strand to alabaster European saints, hence Thomas Merton
petitioned la Virgen de la Caridad del Cobre, asked assistance
with discarding the world's jingbang. From the Sierra Maestra

Fidel Castro rode down into Havana in 1959; in his pockets
a Santeria fetish and a Roman Catholic icon. I've seen white-robed
Santeria priestesses sugar petals in the Hudson's brackish flow.

I witnessed the Mothers of Pocomania, Revival, and Myal trump
the winding way up the Hope River valley; O flocks like blue herons
wing, clean down to dipping pools. For three rainy years I swam

with mermaids captured in paintings I sold for a living. I believe
one might be swimming upstream below the old concrete nog
ivy filigreed cottage where my one son was born: May day.

Rivermummas lap their scale tails in wet caves till hurricanes tear past.

Holy Mother of the sea, what does she there in underwater rooms?
chatelaines a staff of water maids to keep the sea bed washed clean
as the sand floor of Jamaica's great Jewish synagogue.

But in the world pantheon of goddesses Grandy Nanny aces a Valkyrie
or an Amazon; place her atop a cotton tree colonnade, wreath her
in a camouflage crown of quakoo bush; she is to wickedness a great wall

of bounce back; bullets ricocheted off her hinder parts as she lifted
her frock braveheart style and exposed her mighty fortress.
So, Jacob, if you find the griot tell her, tell him, that till I lend

my blacktar skin into whatever earthroad I will be interred; on behalf of
foremother who pushed back downpression through muzzle-tongue of iron,

remember us in motherland.

Hope Gardens

Hope Gardens

You write to immortalize the long-gone
Sunday afternoons light years away by
route of slow silver chi chi omni bus.

Cross Roads   Old Hope   Hope Road,
you in organdy Sunday school dress set
to slip off good shoes and socks and

dash across the green in Hope Gardens;
as the military band in zouave uniforms
sounded brass oompah-pah instruments.

Seated now in a seminar, you're perplexed
as this post-colonial scholar unearths plot
after heinous imperial plot buried behind

our botanical gardens; and you think pity
the people never knew this as we posed
for Brownie camera captured photographs

by flowering trees, or, O joy, showed off
in our wedding dan dan, by lily pond, lay
down ourselves careless in beds of canna

lilies, lost in daydreams of owning own
places with lawns the square of a kerchief.
We the ignorant, the uneducated, unaware,

that the roses we assumed bloomed just
to full eye, were representative of English
lady beauty; unenlightened we were, so we

picked them on the sly to give as token
to the love we got lost in the maze with –
quick thief a kiss – and this colonial design

was nowhere in mind or sight; but even if
and so what? as long as they flung wide
those two-leaved wrought iron double gates

there we would be; gentlemen and ladies all
human beings come in order to draw strength
for the week from our own Hope Gardens.

Quest

At age twelve, six days
        into the start of a year
                this girl was seated

in a whitewashed classroom;
        dreaming herself outdoors
                and up Lignum vitae trees

and heard a teacher read:
        "A cold coming we had of it."
                And just so went on a journey

with men whose names
        or what they went in search of
                never revealed.

She only recalls that when
        a prefect rung the lunch bell
                she was wrenched from the ride

with those men on a quest
        and that she tested on her tongue
                the words "refractory"

and "silken" as adjectives for herself,
        as hints for her own journey; girl exited
                room with vaulted ceiling, disoriented.

Gauguin Girl

"Take me away from this place," she'd ask
the bareback figure astride a grey horse.
The horse pawed the ground, the figure lurked
behind hank of hair blunt down one side of face.
Horse and rider tacked in place on classroom
back wall never invited her to leave the chair
fixed to a desk where she brain-fogged through
long monotonous lessons. Figure did not say

leave this island for a next – Tahiti, where the girls
look like you, and when they are not naked
like ripe fruit rindless, dressed only in hibiscus,
stuck careless by sweat-musk temples.
They wear to conceal their dusk flesh
dresses called "Mother Hubbards," stitched by missionaries.

Our First Christian Martyr

ran the banner headline. News flash;
        she was related to our history teacher.

In morning assembly at St. Hugh's School
        we sung hymns in praise of missionaries

who bear the gospel to heathenlands; hailed
        the brave who risk their lives for Jesus Word

in far areas of darkness for to win dark souls.
        Scenes we pictured in our inward eyes:

her eyes raised to heaven; a hymn winging
        defiant from her lips; savages dragging her

to boiling pot; soundtrack of savage drums
        sound across a jungle where Tarzan was lord

grey smoke rising from torched mission house.
        But before term was over she turned up alive,

saved by natives who spirited her away
        down paths aswarm with armed insurgents.

Down the Congo to the Atlantic where she was
        delivered on to a ship booking out of Africa.

On the day she appeared to show herself to us
       we did not rejoice to see her;

she who deprived us of our first Christian martyr.

My Teacher Lena

They say – I'm not sure – that she now lives in a castle in Denmark.
Surely hers is a medieval castle with stone walls yards deep.
I visited Sweden in 1990 during the summer solstice.
The windows were blindless; the sun would not set.
I attempted to outstare it.

And I dined on schools of herring and small boiled potatoes
blue-white like opals and bought in a market, a paper bag
of cherries I ate all at one go as I sat on a park bench
to meditate upon Hans Christian Andersen
as played by Danny Kaye.

When I cobblestoned my way back to the bed and breakfast
where I stayed it had turned into a brick box of scandal
as the teenaged daughter of the owner – who was away
on vacation – decided to run off with
her mother's boyfriend.

He of the sad countenance and the ten-month pregnant paunch
whose hair was sparse; it was all very Ingmar Bergman.
While I was there I thought I'd go visit my teacher
in her castle; because in my atlas, Denmark
and Sweden are twinned

hence I'd be able to skip briskly across a fjord of connecting ice.
But the teenaged mess of a girl inside me blubbered how
she might not remember the overweight sixth former
who told her I wanted to read books with characters
who looked and sounded more like me.

And she'd said, "You are a writer; write what you want to read."

Reading Through the Wall

My inner life; my sovereign state
became like the maze in Hope Gardens,
shrivelled, upon my father's death.

As did my intention of inviting him
to dine at a high-class restaurant
where I would foot the bill
from my first paycheque.

As we'd long abandoned the band
your belly and bawl out grief
practice of our Guinea foremothers,

my family worked
it through ourselves.

I was sent to live with my sister
in her new house in the foothills
of the Blue Mountains.

It was there in the library
I found volumes belonging to
my brother-in-law's once intended,
who'd read English;

I opened with Sir Gawain
O hurt of a lost head.

Moved to Chaucer and then
on to Shakespeare's sonnets.
By the time I reached Matthew Arnold

I considered myself
a scholar Gypsy.

But it was really John Donne
who acted on my grief. I confesss
I could not puzzle all his extravagant
conceits; but trying worked free

the bound roots of my within,
made it receptive to the clean wash
of George Herbert – who like my father
was a kind man – to do regenerative work.

His lemonbalm words warmed
and quickened my pulse points when
I hymned from the Book of Common Praise;

soaring with his lyrics to heaven or
the cool green hills of Malvern
where I imagined my father returned.

Wherefore with my utmost art/I will sing thee
And the cream of all my heart/I will bring thee.

I crooned too Ben Jonson's delicate airs.

Drink to me only with thine eyes and I will pledge with mine

I spooned Rev. Herbert's cream,
tippled Ben's wine, abandoned
all else and read through that brick wall of texts.

Mostly hardcover, almost all by men,
so when I came to Edna St. Vincent Millay
I all but hugged her slim paperback,

a woman's voice a woman's voice, determined
to recreate her riotous all-night ride
upon the Ferry, got up a big group of friends,

lollygagged down to Kingston Harbour,
rode the old launch over to Port Royal,
then wrote an imitation of "Renascence."

Poignant musings on resurrection
and death. I woke next day and tore it up.
I may even have set it ablaze
on a makeshift funeral pyre
along with a pile of my other early efforts.

Bookmobile Days

The one who was pressed
up against the door
clutching the last book borrowed;
book read by naked light bulb,
street lamp, bottle torch, or moonlight.

The child who'd cut ties
to blood lines and school friends
in order to make the acquaintance
of characters bound to become
trusted lifelong companions.

That one would brave blizzards,
extract swords from stones,
fly back to Guinea never ever
having eaten salt.
Fall in and out of doomed love,
forget tethered goats,
neglect to fetch water
in a tin that once brought kerosene
and so draw the ire of parents.
This is the one who would
climb aboard wide-eyed and greedy
for what was carried in the hold
of our brave new world caravel on wheels.

She said: "I'd like a book of fairy tales please."
It was a weekday
but she was all Sunday clothes.
Pink frilly frock   butterfly bows
white socks   patent leather shoes.
She said her godmother had dressed her up
to come and visit the bookmobile.

Tagore on the Bookmobile

If it is not my portion to meet thee in this my life
then let me ever feel that I have missed thy sight
         — RABINDRANATH TAGORE, *Gitanjali*

Belly full of books enough to sustain you on your journey
all of a hundred miles in a day to far outposts
of your father's parish.

To small school houses where "*belleng*" bellenged
the handheld bell, when great giving bookmobile
toiled into view

schoolchildren heralding its coming

Bookmobile come, the bookmobile come.

Gitanjali, you found between *A Child's Garden of Verses*
and *The Oxford Book of Modern Verse*; lyrics that shivered
your head top off.

Watered your gaze on the clay red landscape.

What hard love was this Tagore spoke of? Pitiless force
able to gouge unhealable gash in the heart; like mined-out
bauxite quarries the machine heaved past.

Flesh could not sustain such feelings as the poet spawned;
you would fall but come to see how all echoed the Friend's
name; all of it Beloved's surrogate.

At days end wending home past the balm yard flags
you would feel yourself stream out toward Him;
and all because of Tagore of Bengal.

Town Drunk Recites Omar Khayyam

The drunkalready, as the bookmobile passes
calls out: "A flask of wine, a book of verse
and thou beside me there in the wilderness";

Then he salaams, folds his soused self in half.
Somehow his old rude boy hat stays fixed
does not fall off even as the whiterum wafts

and weaves about him, near tangible shade,
can almost be seen arising from flat-sided
Appleton rum flask. This liquor inflames,

harsh ways overproof spirit has; torch
of buildings, cut of heartstrings, carry wide
of poor man with a little knowledge. Omar

you might want to explain something to this
liquor bibber, charmed so by your quatrains
carried over by Fitzgerald, you'd be remiss

if you did not clarify whether all that wine
the tent maker imbibed was pressed hard
from grapes grown on earth vines or spirit.

Need

The one time I smoked   a rizzla-rolled spliff
              in my green youth

I hung suspended   by a nerve sling of panic;
              from the rooftops

After I came down   smoke nought but plain tobacco.
              I made a vow:

Though I imbibed some wine   the hip state of California
              to cultivate

I distilled in my mindless   I scribe of hard times
              spirit fruit place

subsistence farming nothing   on Blue Mountain hillside
              but small yield grapes

poor harvest of that arbour   beg outside Omar's tavern
              sometimes made me

where I saw a writer woman   before her doting audience.
              stumbledrunk

Listen to me, my children   the art of picking up hints.
              I recommend this:

Saw me in her if I kept at it.   I'll bid goodbye to edge-teeth
              Before leaving earth

drinks; take instead bitters to   eat honey so I speak sweet
                    purify the palette

whenever I raise a cup filled   is this what Khayyam meant?
                    with thanks and praise

Tea. I'll take in multiple cups   for me in gratitude to savour.
                    this is wine enough

But the Friend I need, oh how I need, the Beloved every hour.

In the Blue Boarding House

In the Blue Boarding House

Many poets are not poets for the same reason that religious men and women are
not saints; they never succeed in being themselves. They never get around to
being the particular poet or the particular monk [or nun] they are intended to be
by God. They never become the man [or woman] or the artist who is called for
by all the circumstances of their life. They waste their years in vain efforts to be
some other poet or some other saint.

— THOMAS MERTON

i

Take it as I tell you; every surface there was a shade
from baby to midnight in that big old rented house.
Totally blue, even the wind-up Smith alarm clock

which clock-work went off at six when she'd rouse us
with her signature reveille: "Good Morning Heartache
Here We Go Again" round and round the gramophone.

New boarders would softshoe past her bedroom door,
converse in hushed tones, pretend to avert their eyes
from last night's still life laid careless out on the tiles:

Slipper satin evening dress pooled to glaze meltdown.
Lace garter belt hooked to silk stockings, stiletto heels,
white flower pristine by bag with bloody syringe.

We who hadn't signed leases were savvy enough not
to touch her stuff; we got high on scald black coffee
and sung her praises in friend-up notes: last night's show

was fabulous! your very best yet! I'm your biggest fan!
If you could not make rent she'd make you run errands
do her laundry, press her dresses, cook her meals.

She took her supper hot to burn excess off her voice box.
High yellow, she craved greens; said of steamed
spinach: "Even the food I like most is half blue."

Life there was one long low residency program for ones
aspiring to live somebody else's life done lived.
Miss lady owned the cream gardenia; you? no flower.

Then raise high the roofbeams the Beloved came flying
pennants that spelled "time to abandon these premises"
I seized the day and booked; booked, ended my stay.

Dropped blue keys into once red mailbox now indigo
after brewing her a pot of Blue Mountain coffee, I split,
wrote her a left-handed note: "Not my life, this XX."

      ii

The real reason I left: looked out from my attic window
in time to see national enquirer throw-word tour bus
pull up across the street.

Tour Guide: "Over here you see lady's house of tragedy."
Through deaf-ears screams and blind of flashbulbs, Beloved
parted the crowd.

My Dear One who'd come to spirit me from the mansion
of perpetual mashdown had a pencil behind one ear –
I write with it right now –

took a stance, aimed clean hands, flags shot from blunt
fingers and signalled: time to abandon blue premises,
move from these premises.

I grabbed my exercise book and ran out into the street,
True Friend and me, jumped revival; I shook my frocktail
at the tour bus bitches.

"Let's leave this place," Sweetheart said, head for Heartease.
We set out to go right through right through the rocky road
but the higher we went

the more the air thinned, as did my breath. "Find your second
wind of faith," Love said, so I gasped, "I believe, I believe"
right then a grey mule dainty-stepped

right up (more anon about that mule), and we mounted and
climbed till we reached the flat, atop of a high mountaintop
of, as you would say, a plateau.

Beloved: "The blue house is a place to visit, why live in it?"
Because my mind is contrary and divided. I want to be
sweetheart to loverman and holy to Paraclete.

From and to and to and from All Saints Sunday school
              I passed their meetings; parson said they were
                        nothing but uncouth heathen unChristian pagans.

Still I was moved so by those loose-limb moves
            faces oiled up, eyeballs rolled way back in socket
                        made poem's later talk of inward eye spell sense.

Desire rose in me to echo their loud glory-trumpet
            shouts, I'd swallow hard when bidden to stand
                        stock still and mechanical pipe hymns from a pew.

Or kneel to be always led in prayer by the minister
            who is remembered not for uplifting sermons, just
                        for how he'd prostrated himself in the centre aisle

to demonstrate the prone position of that traveller
            who had fallen among thieves; the man redeemed
                        by a good Samaritan; that was the same clergyman

who'd rebuked me, said I was prone to causing
            commotions whenever I entered Sunday school.
                        So I tried thereafter to speak softly and to train

my eyes upon this crucifix: a lifesized black Christ cut
            and carved from a struck-by-lightning ebony tree;
                        to whom I squeezed out petitions: O Dear Lord

Do Lord, help me never more to cause commotions.
            May I grow into a woman pure chaste virtuous
                        as Virgin Mary and not an old harlot like Jezebel.

Going home one Sunday I was witness to this drama:
            A band of Africans jumping poco in the streets
                        and a church mother in the grip of the Paraclete.

It pitched her down flat, ripped off her red tie head
                wiped it across the concrete, hiked her long gown
                                to expose shine thighs that scissored and cut

clean the slip knot that bound spirit to sense.
                O My God! Is that what will happen to me?
                  I stood in my shoes and I wondered.

That my white dress was not more bridal gown
                was my main concern as I took first communion.
                          Confirmed, this girl felt nothing, not the merest breath

the Holy Spirit, for it whooshed past me at the altar rail
                to anoint with a kiss the brow of good girlchild
                        who did not in secret aspire to be a nightclub singer.

O to be a torch singer denizen of smoky places,
                dolled up in ruched satin gowns, bee-stung lips
                        stained rubyred by Max Factor, ah the slow burn

siren style of exquisite evening attire, the affect
                of set struck pose so languid yet set to run race
                        of hard running women of the racehorse ankles.

Dreamy eyes veiled half closed by cigarette smoke.
                Ai to make moan about a man done gone and left
                  a lady at daybreak to tell heartache good morning.

This way of being I came by honestly; from English literature:
                my father – player of instruments wind and string –
                  and six brothers who spun vinyl: 78   33⅓   45.

A girlchild whose one ambition was to be a big woman.

        To perform in concert with Sarah   Ella   Billie   Dinah.

           To become denizen of nightclub, to sing for my supper

where O where can you be, loverman or Paraclete?

        In the presence of all the Saints I made this petition:

           Come o come breathe on me and let me be a cantatrice.

"Not song but its sweetheart poetry is your way to Heartease.

        It will come on wings viewless to lift you

           from scorch way of torch singers long slow burning

and turn your wayward gaze from Billie Holiday's cream

        gardenias brought fresh by night blooming admirers."

        But that answer only made me want to croon:

A Small Blues for Lady's Gardenia

Mixed signals sent
scent sensual
yet nunlike

wide open
light bloom
worn off
to one side.

wide lotus
a float on
dark waters
of song

little girl blue
wanted to wear
one too.

Dance Card

Come Saturday night, we five, including
Tom Yew who was all of 6 ft 4
jammed into a Morris mini-minor

borrowed from my sister; till one day
I bought and paid for one of my own
(for which I am thankful)

for one should not always a borrower be.

Hers was egg white, mine a pat of butter;
neat cube-shaped little loaf cakes
they were, those sweet cars.

Before I bought mine we'd comandeer
my sister's so Tom Yew, Glenda
Howard and Patrick and me could

bubble down the hill into Glass Bucket
or swashbuckle through
the Bucaneer lounge

where the waiters sported pirate uniforms
and this expat cockney band
called the Pearly Kings banged on.

We ourselves were partial to the mellow
of soulful Richard Ace and his trio
but mostly

we wanted the live music to take a break
and so allow the deejay who was
not in those days

a rapper, but a selector, who spun discs
so we could shuffle and spin
too, proud we were

of our as yet unbroken record of never once
sitting out a song, we girls
and boys of the dance;

linked together in a jump-up ring;
loud warbling along to Sparrow's
slack calypso lyrics.

Groovers were we to sweet-soul rhythm
and blues, also local music, which
then was ska

and how did we know that one day ska
would settle down into rocksteady
quicken into reggae and rule?

We always loved our music though;
did not miss a beat; legs we legsed
and did we not drop-foot?

We shut every night spot down;
passing by churchgoers risen
with dawn, we faded home.

Haul and pull up just one more time
again; could my four old friends
of the dance and me

rev that little mini-minor engine down
the incline of Gordon Town hillside
and by small moons of headlights

shine our way into a spot wherein
to dominate the floor till the band
or deejay cries "*Cree*,"

leaving us soaped in sweat, but keen
in case Mr. Music for old time's sake
consents to lick it from the top again.

Otis Ode

The strong young men called on Otis to beg for them
plead for them out there on the dangerous dance floor.

Implore Otis to ask a girl permission to press up close
and rent a tile, pretending this was their wedding dance.

The boys depended solely on Otis to convince pretty
girls born with knowledge that beauty controlled

the quick sap rising in trembling awkward striplings;
out on a limb as voices broke on a take a chance:

"Care to dance?" Youth man breathing hard waits for
the verdict: one "no thanks" or a "I'm too tired" but

with the advocacy of Otis they had hope she'd say
"Yes" and so allow hot clammy hand-hold privilege.

Grateful boy walks girl onto dance floor, palm slides
to small of back, tries to lead slow dance; girl shuts

eyes tight and projects her ripe self to rub up close
against hunky hard body of handsome Otis Redding.

Nomenclature come straight up from Georgia clay.
O Redding, son of Macon, Georgia, what's in the water

there to make Little Richard, James Brown, Hoagy
Carmichael, and Michael Stipes to all be of Macon?

Where this day I've come to look for Otis to see
his bronzed self statued there down by the Ocmulgee

River; I followed the sound of into the Georgia Music
Hall of Fame where the display tells how he did well

for himself, was gifted, made money, owned the big O.
I like that photograph of you seated astride your horse.

You wrote your own songs, one on the back of a bill.
RESPECT, Otis wrote that, Aretha owned it, he said

all the SUCCESS she had with it was fine with him,
he was thriving. It was not always so, here we see

evidence of the sing slow bite your tongue years.
He carried baggage of, hefted band equipment for,

drove a station wagon taking others to sound studios;
till one day he begged for himself extra session time

left over by a small-scale singer, and O stepped up
to the mike, and as fans today would say: Killed!

It is recorded that in respect due when he met Otis
in Kingston in 1979, Bob Marley stood and chanted

"These Arms of Mine"

Old school, I was in the crowd hailing you then, hail
you now. Otis Redding, advocate of all love's beggars.

Paul Robeson at Athena's

Me

Council of the mighty, seat of the powerful
are not places for a one like me; I'm more the kind
who sits in the kitchen and swaps recipes with cook.

Athena

Just like Paul Robeson who dined with the premier
after his recital at the Carib Theatre, heads of state at his feet,
yet who did he ask to meet with? The domestic help.

Tall on the kitchen table, crown of his head just shy
of the crown moulding, Paul serenaded cooks & maids
with praise anthems to deserving workers of the world.

Me

One of the many differences between the great Paul
And nobody me – I grew big with child; I quit politics.

Athena

Accept this invitation to drinks at my salon where Rilke
run-jostles with Samora Machel and William Blake bests
Kapo, even as two sevens clash: green bell   orange head.

Me

This is the poem I never did write while you lived.
My sincere thanks as beneficiary of your noblesse oblige,
your back veranda a tiled oasis of gin and tonic civility.

You opened your studio and invited me to contemplate
a life lived in service to art; poem I never wrote to you
who when my artistic efforts took off & crossed salt water,

was enraged; for you'd allowed how my fate was to spend
turn-my-hand days, practising local craft. Who sent a spider
I don't know, but I might have been tongue-tied by the bite. I was not.
Give thanks, give thanks, give thanks.

Red T-Shirt

Here is a photo of you in a barbwire-fenced field.
You're dressed in jeans and a red T-shirt; it reads
"Forward to Full Socialism."

It was taken at a rally of the party's Women's
Movement; maybe called the "Women's Arm"
then, you don't remember.

All you recall was it was a rainy October day
and you rode to the rally with a politician
and a brigadista not long from Cuba.

And you mounted a display of photographs.
Glossy prints of sugar co-ops or working-class
women working construction.

Earlier you'd stopped and attended a meeting
in a hall; a Jamaica Welfare community centre
named for Norman Manley, Fabian socialist

who'd appealed to the conscience of the United
Fruit Company to donate a fraction of one percent
of a year's profits to the welfare of our peasants.

But that day in the 1970s when you were wrapped
in the red flag as a T-shirt, Manley's party
was lurching forward – or so it was thought –

to full socialism. What exactly did that mean?
Even the manifesto was approximate.
Still many of the comrades were fully committed

to our *social living* experiment that we were
certain would succeed, after all our cause was just.

But things did not end well. No, my comrade.
The last revolutionary ninety miles from here
is now an old lion, the same one

we vowed to follow to the mountaintop where
the Japanese now cultivate Blue Mountain coffee
and the IMF, like the poor, are still with us.

The Two Sisters Cave

A half-remembered Taino legend claims the two figures split from one rock
                    were once blood sisters
                    in a cave hiding out

from the bloodhounds of the conquerers, from horrid contagion come
                    sudden upon them when not
                    long before they were

sudding the white froth root of cassava, free of its take-life toxicity.
                    I like to imagine the two could have
                    been me and my sister

in past times when she and I in loving tendermercy kept company;
                    each to each supplying salt and light's
                    vital support.

We (both being action figures) might have projected ourselves to the shore
                    and stopped up the holes in Columbus's
                    rickety old boats

so he and his band of wreck sailors would have waked to find their holey
                    barks seaworthy; and set sail again
                    in pursuit of elusive gold fields

leaving us in peace. My sister and me. If we'd made peace in that cave
                    instead of all this *Whatever Happened to Baby Jane?*
                    instead of all trying in vain to convert strangers into
                    sisters
                    who knows how our people's story would now read.

Your Heart

the Beloved said, is like a hotel.
So many rooms so many suites
occupied by unreal interests.

My backanswer:
I am trying to live my parents' dream
of operating a first-rate guest house.

That was their vision, what is yours?

To restore to spotless the wasted years
of canker worm and gnawing locusts.

To represent scroll of new Psalms I ate
and committed to memory's keepsafe.

To ensure my son will never sit down
on a sidewalk and beg from Babylonians.

That can only be done when
the alone meets the alone
heart as hotel shut down; move on.

Bye Boonoonoonoos

Bye Boonoonoonoos

Bye to the bird
of the most accurate
shade of chartreuse
which used to trill from a crossbeam

in the kitchen; kiss,
blow a kiss to that one
arthritic rose bush
mixture of rose madder, salmon pink

and maroon that
would extend a single
bloom as welcome
back to your boy, his best friend of a dog

and the hushabye of the river.
Before now you could not let
yourself record its teardown,
and your son asking mother why? why can't we

just go home? But
those were those days
thank love; love prevailed,
cottage kept up by ivy, hemmed round by bush,

cedar leaf fall
and euphorbia, foreshadow
of actual ice and snow.
Bye Boonoonoonoos cottage of poems shook down.

One in a Long Line

Substance of things hoped for
no amount of if at first and try try
and try again could obtain.

Pulled up stakes without even a
"Go and good go with you
and take this heel of hardough

bread for the journey, accept tot
of whiterum and sop it spirit
skullcap against mole cold."

Went anyway. Became one in
a long line of alien gleaners
who bear the icon of Mary

taking the boy to Egypt for safety.
Called out to Hagar how you too
were mother of a boychild

and you were both in want of a well.
Applied to Khadija wife of the prophet
for a job in the buy and sell business.

Held always before you examples
of sojourning women going far
for substance of things hoped for.

Our Blessed Country Lady

From my brown cup freckled
        with white dots
                I'd sip mint or fevergrass tea
fresh or sweetened with
spoonful of logwood honey
and I'd watch for our Blessed Country Lady.

She who carried a load
        on her head, usually a pile
                of the island's crosses
she'd elected to bear
for the ones who could not
manage them themselves.

No matter how my own day
        had been, whether or not
                a poem came or a painting
or a job to pay the rent,
I'd greet her as she descended
the side of the mountain;

shifting those burdens slow so
        dark did not fall all at once,
                she'd hail me back, say
"Thanks for the greeting;
I would love to come in
and see what you do today

but I am on haste; for I
   have to take this dirty bundle
     down to the river and wash

it out to sea; that way
when morning come again
some can start over clean."

On Sighting Makak by the Roadside

Stopping by the road from Vieux Fort Airport
we sight Makak; statue of coal by a culvert,
palming a green orb of a water jelly coconut.

Makak cutlassed the husk top off, I locked lips
with it and let its waters flood my throat,
let it soak my thick grey clothes.

Environmentalists put out his tree burning;
hence the coconut stand by the highway.
No, he didn't want foreign money.

The driver took the U.S. dollars and paid Makak
in local currency. Rinsed, I felt, heartwashed
as I sat back in the van's back seat.

I knew at once that this was what
I'd needed to see, the moment I saw this:

a woman of a certain age, her forehead gelled
with aloes, prostrate out on the tamped dirt
floor of her one-room house.

I needed to do that. Aiee, take low and so allow
cinders in my flesh to drop into engine room
at earth centre; to let fall

from mind and body; slings, arrows caught in me.
I wanted to do a painting of the woman.
I'd favour purple in my palette, I'd title it:

Earth's Mother Bathed Her with Fresh Livity.
The cotton balls on the kapok trees spun
white outside the van,

blew backwards toward Vieux Fort and polished
the wings of the Delta flight lifting
off for the land of ice.

The Bear
for Ted

There he was; great bear of my dreams
crossing the road just outside Gibsons
in no particular hurry;

like a long-legged pigeon-toed man
with a gait presidential; bopping cool.
Bear just ambled, slightly shambolic
dipped in front of the car, my heart leapt.
You, love, were hoping I had not seen it.

I did. But wasn't scared as I imagined
I'd be upon my first bear sighting.

Ursa, down from the evening sky slipped
through the bank of pine trees; never broke
even one branch; for him, the green parted.

Last night the bear was dancing in a ring
With our children;
I called to you "Papa, come quick,
the kids aren't aware that it's a bear
they're cavorting with."

But they seemed comically happy out there
and the bear tra la la'd across Halfmoon Bay.

Now the bear enters into our living room
where our lamp shaped like a horse waits
to be unpacked;

I shoo it with a damp dish cloth. It shows
no sign of being even one bit perturbed

and I wonder if the bear is thinking
of moving in, if he will sit in our armchairs,
eat up our porridge.

A New State

i

Rembrandt reworked the worn plate;
burnished away figures, established
new ones, crosshatched curtains
of dark over light areas.

The three crosses;
the Christ and the two thieves remain.

The crowd comes and goes.
The mob bawling "crucify him"
will outnumber those once dumb
whose tongues he loosed;

who now withhold their new found
powers of speech.

The ones walking, halt no more,
he told get up and get going; stand still.

Eyes he stung open with salt of his spit;
squint to see which way the vote will swing;

The zealot Barabas the Christ Jesus

Rembrandt
on different days caused the number
of believers to outweigh those against.
Somedays believers win.

ii

Lift the old print
from the mount
that's become worn.

Use a scalpel
to slit the guards
holding old print
down.

Freed from guards
mend print's tears
and weak areas
with wheat
(not tares)
starch paste.

Press print lightly
between clean
blotting paper
and weighted boards
for removal of any
or all undulations.

That done, attach
new margin
termed "false"
– which means
in this case
a new one
as opposed
to worn original.

This is called
"a new state."

Every step
in the restoration
process
is a new state.

iii

Sacred wound
gouge
of hard love
heals into gift
cicatrice

aches to warn
when you brush
too close
to flesh excess

shellacs into
scarab beetle
tracking
back and forth
setting off
monitor and
alarm

go home
go home via
silence inroads
to heartcave.
There you
dwell safe.

What Does It Mean

What does it mean when
Ali Baba's forty thieves
accuse you of being dishonest?

When Macbeth's witches
stir up double trouble
and add you?

When sad circus freak
claims you and them are in
sideshow as conjoined twins.

When a bum on the bus
assumes you're both bound
for Florida to panhandle.

When latchkey children
insist on mistaking your
front door for their own.

It means, my love, you're being
polished into a mirror; aiee,
you sob, there's the rub.

Everyday Revelations

i

The newly departed ring you on the telephone.
They do not reply to: hello hello.

They morph into force, flinging coins from your purse.
They become source of hope, coppers for the luckless.

The just buried become "things" magnets;

Rigor limbs stiff halves of paired earrings
body snatch one-foot of socks, widow saucers of cups.

Who do you think just knocked
yet when you opened the door there was
only that used rose and snapped stems of baby's breath?

ii

The white horse will canter past footwalkers.
There is a chance we will arrive after
all those robes of white have been handed out.

The filthy might – just as John decreed – be filthy still.
You see that is what is not right with big revelations;
there is no room for redemptions at the last minute.

Like this:
For ones like us, great-grandmother will come mounted
on her broad-backed grey mule to canter us skyward
where like schoolchildren we'll line up to get gold stars.

iii

Blue blouse of recycled sari cloth
stitched by women in a co-op; money paid
– says label – goes to help women in a village.

Wide silk sleeves billow, allspice drifts,
my mother's hand adjusts shoulder's fit.
Pray this:

May the seamstresses share of this purchase
be enough for this day's rice and peas.

iv

In the waiting room at the dentist
I read *National Geographic*;
but I'm not appalled by the sight
of naked large-breasted natives
who resemble me and my own relatives.
One art Miss Bishop.

I read and digest instead a feature
on water taxis of Burma.
How the saffron sails are stitched

from used robes of monks.
How the currents are fragrant with prayers
as the junks sail.

     v

A blackbird full-stops the end of a branch
weights it into a straight line.
To the right margin, pinnate leaves
a series of dashes.
The mountains go high as seven thousand
feet, wet grass gleams at morning.
White egrets wheel.

Mountains say:

You went away but see we stayed
we remain your place to hide in
your source of blue stone
to heal hurt; slate and chalk
to write to graft marble vein
into endure of heart.

You were gone too long, say mountains.

She went far, very far, says breeze.

She was cold, says red water grass.

Warm her, says flame of the forest.

Morning Ballad

Shift into first as you ascend old Stony Hill.
The good mother will dispatch heaven scent
of baking bread to revive you in the valley
when it drops down.

You will pass a school walled only on one side.
The vendors of fruit: pineapples, ortaniques
will tumble over themselves to get to your car.

Buy a sugarloaf pineapple peeled into a plastic bag.

Here your return starts; do not pause again except
to bless yourself if chicken hawks cross overhead
or a sly mongoose skids into the cane brakes.

Head for the concrete nog house past the old ties
of train line; the one with a red-brick floor kitchen
and the cut stone fire wall along all four sides.

The renk from the goat pen will water your eyes.

Reach to Golden Spring; sing morning ballad.
Spirit sankeys have no tone; wordless you went,
heart full of nightingale lament from this place.

Now you wonder how, why your feet strayed,
what made you go away from an island where
someone named a wayside cottage: "Morning Ballad."

Not that you did not strive, try to remain, to settle
in one spot and deep-root like these trees that romp
with storms winds; spit back at blow hard hurricanes.

Mourning Ballad to those years; what dark ways
you went, loss and sad songs your best friends.

"Mother, why are you sadding?"

       Sadding into grace state or something like it.
       Voice stretched elastic can contralto sorrow,
       ululate praise, bridge broken re-establish
       pass to Heartease.

A Cleanse Petition

Our Lady of Sorrows.

Our Lady Star of the Sea.

Our Lady of Banana Walks

Our Lady of stately palm trees

tall once again after lethal

yellow, cut-down disease.

Our Lady of rain on the waves

Our Lady filler of fishing seines

Our Lady of gown of cobalt blue,

wash our hearts,

do cleanse blood spill of innocents

who lose their heads.

Cleanse the ground we tread

from ground in grime of violence.

Our Lady of Remedies.

Note to Self

Go to Goldeneye, visit with Chris Blackwell.
Music never had a better best friend.

Tour the rooms, touch the desk where Ian Fleming
launched James Bond with the swagger
of a Jamaican fisherman.

Near here Honey Ryder rose like Venus from the waves.
In a brief bikini she dived for conch shells
to sell, she said, in Miami.

She was singing a ditty no Jamaican ear had ever heard
about underneath the mango tree, she and her
honey making boolooloo.

Oracabessa home of honey light that limns
all around with gold leaf; could this be the city
sought after by prophets and poets?

Could this town by the sea Columbus named
for gold he sought but never found here
be the fabled city?

               Moveable feast. The city of gold
               is everywhere you have ever been.

In the city of gold, bright souls gather
and wash face, hands, and limbs
in light so liquid, it can be poured from water glasses.

This light that burnishes, travels and arrives
ahead of you, wherever you go where Good sends you.

By the gold oil light of a curry goat lunch
by the rose-gold of a refill fruit punch
laugh off the low tricks of the wicked.

And turn thanks, turn thanks in hummingbird thrum
to this land where you were born reluctant poet
painter who gessoed her voice with pebbledash

and scrawled with a blot-prone pen-nib leaking
quick ink, shadowing in the tops of all e's
and tore dark holes in paper to swallow words
but somehow, somehow, poet, here you are.
Still on the road to Heartease; the city of gold
is the site of Heartease. Journeys.

Charlie Chaplin at Golden Clouds

Charlie Chaplin declared Oracabessa
Paradise. One hundred and one years ago
on this day, time stood still there for him.

At Golden Clouds he smiled and checked
in for a time his bag of crosses carried
from childhood; bag of abandonment and

want that made him identify with the poor
little man; baggypants, coat too tight, castoff
shoes so outsized, he wore them right to left.

Cane and a bowler hat, wicked man's mock
moustache. Jesus, what a job! Responsibility
for making this world laugh. Chaplin

looked out silently from his room window
framing the Caribbean Sea and saw rowing
hard, big fishermen who cannot swim.

He went for a walk and watched banana
men dressed like tramps, cultivating
acres of hillside land. The inheritors of earth

about their business, not caring about who
the great man was, except to offer him a jelly
coconut – Oracabessa sun can be hot – or like

the chambermaid, recite a psalm as she turned
down his clean sheets that he'd pass the night
in peace; to rise up come morning rested.

Canto I

for Derek Walcott

Halfway through the journey of my life
        I come to find myself in a wild rocky place
for to tell you the truth my feet had strayed.

Tongue cannot tell how this place was hard
        just to talk of it make me frighten all over again.
Bitter! Barren! Only death itself could be worse,

but the price I paid for my survival is this:
        I am now must and bound to tell you of the good
that I found down there; well ma'am, well sir

how I reached down there it is hard to tell
        but my mind was mixed-up contrary divided
and I slip-slide away from the right path

so that I find myself at the foot of a mountain
        at the end of a stony valley where what I saw
nearly caused my heart to attack me in my chest.

I look up and to see the shoulder of the mountain
        burnished with early morning sun beams that guide
the pure in heart as they go along their way

and when I see this my fear was dampened a bit
        So that the panic that had pitched and tossed me
the night before, tossed me to my core, abated.

Like a swimmer who is out of her depth in big sea,
	who battle the waves until she reach to shore
and as she blow for breath she marvel at how

she managed to escape from grave watery death.
	Just like that, I turned back to study with awe
the dark pass that no one before me had left alive.

And as I catch up my exhausted self I began to climb
	up the rocky mountainside making sure to place
my foot where it would not slip and cause me to fall

when lo and behold on the side of the mountain
	a leopardess! pardner, her foot light, it swift!
her skin like white dominoes spotted with black ink.

She was shuffling there staring straight into my face.
	Blocked, she try to block my every step so all I could
do was feint and move sideways. It was just before day

remember now; the morning sun was rising up to take
	its place among the late staying stars that surrounded
Love divine whose hand connected the great lights

and set them on high to shine, ah, the before day hours
	the soft doctor breeze that caused me to feel hopeful
that I could conquer the ferocious fanged spotted beast.

But that hope was to prove weak; not strong enough
	to overcome my fear when I saw come tearing down
toward me a lion! massive dread, hungry driving him

like a big engine so that even the breeze blow like it
            was afraid. Then a she-wolf, she lurking beside him
craven, scrawny, maugre you could see white squall

at her mouth corner and you know that she had caused
            many to suffer and to feel it. The sight of her broke
my spirit, I just gave up right there any hope of being

able to climb up that mountain, just like someone
            who is a wordlian who one day loses all his or her
earthly possessions and falls rightaway into despair

and faint spirit overtakes them, makes them give up
            I became like that in the presence of the awful beast
bearing down the mountain upon me step by step.

And when I was beating my retreat to lower ground
            before my frightened eyes a man suddenly appeared
his voice was calm and low like he'd long been silent.

And when I saw him in that terrible place I cried out
            help me do   pity me   whoever you may be
whether living man or a May Pen duppy, do help me.

He answered me: I am not a man though once I was.
            I come from good parents my father was an artist
my mother a schoolteacher I was born after Victoria

sat long upon her throne I was one of the first at the college
            of Mona where the great minds of our archipelego
(along with mediocre) came to be trained in their day.

I am a poet, painter, and playwright founder of the finest
        band of thespians ever collected in the Caribbean,
maybe not just there but anywhere actors tread the boards.

But why are you going back down to strife and woe?
        Why don't you keep climbing upward to the higher
heights of these mountains? up to the source of all joy?

Are you, Sir, the great fountainhead of inspiration
        from whom such a river of creativity flowed?
I asked of him – my head in respect due-bowed low.

Sir, you are the most gifted of our poets and playwrights
        in the name of my faithful study of your books
my love for you and your love of excellence, help me please.

You were my guide and mentor and it is from your example
        that I have crafted this style for which
people worldwide now give me speak; do you see that beast

that I am running from? please, please protect me from her
        O illustrious poetman, for my blood is trembling in
my veins with fear; trembling even as I am standing up here.

You are going to have to take a different path, he said
        if you want to make your way out of this bitter place
for that ferocious beast that is making you so terrified

she does not allow anyone to succeed or pass her by
        she stands and blocks the road, she kills passersby
her nature is so vile so grasping so run-gainst so bad mind

her appetite can never be satisfied, even a belly full
                only makes her hungrier; she has made alliances
with many other wild-natured bloodsuckers just like her

and she will continue in this way until such time when
                the great one, who'll not eat down the riches
of these lands, but will feed us on love and wisdom, comes.

This great one will be saviour of our besieged Caribbean
                the one for whom Grandy Nanny, Marcus Garvey,
and all our other mighty freedom fighters were preparing us

in every village, town, and city across this arc of islands.
                The great one will drive the beast back until she goes
down again to hell from where envy sent her to plague us.

Right now it is best for you to come follow behind me.
                I will direct and guide you, lead you through this place
that is godforsaken, where you will hear cries of woe

where you will witness ancestral spirits in their grief
                bawling out how they have not died once but twice over.
You will look also on the ones who have determinded to stay

in the purifying flames for they hope one day to rise clean
                and join – wherever they may be – the host of pure and holy.
But if you wish to reach up to the seventh level of heaven

there is a soul worthier than I who can take you up there,
                I will leave you in her care when I depart, for the ruler
of the higher heights above forbids that I who rebelled

against all forms of hierarchy and divisions of class and race,
        should approach unto that elevated place of state.
No, the straw bosses who rule these places and sit on high

Say, "We and we alone decide who will fall and who will rise."
        Hear me: O great poet I beseech you by the Most High
with whom you wrestled so, do, help me that I may know how

to fly from this wickedness and worse, lead me wherever
        you said that we should go just now, so that I may stand
one day in the presence of Brother Peter, heaven's gatekeeper

and those lost souls you say that are bowed down so low
        with grief and who are in need of comfort and hope.
And so it was he moved on: I marked well his footsteps.

Soon It Is Going To Rain Milk

Ruth

Orpah said her version of what will be will be
as she stepped away from the old woman;
there was a falling action. This

in response to Naomi's overwrought speech
about there being no more sons in her womb
for her widowed daughters-in-law to marry.

Orpah threw up her hands and turned towards
the land from whence she'd come, to return
as woman living on sufferance of resentful relatives.

But Ruth, Ruth she spoke timely words:
entreat me not to leave thee, whither thou goest.
Who knew our Ruth was a poet

whose name would be sounded across the ages,
cited as model for loyalty and faithfulness,
or that her last state would be greater than her first?

That she'd marry Boaz; owner of wheat fields
she'd gleaned in, and so become matriarch of the line
of David, celebrated king and eminent psalmist.

And that a young poet who was soon to spit blood
would put pen to paper and summon up Ruth
to bear witness to birdsong in fields of alien corn
where we are all, every one of us, far from home.

Hagar's Account

Bring my food. Fetch me water.
Make my bed.

Her next order was an imperative set
to the accompaniment of brass bracelets;
and a hitch of her skirts.

I order you to lie with my husband.

She who had everything was barren.
She who would be denied nothing
would have a child. Mine.

She watched as her husband, head of the tribe,
entered my body. I did not move.

      She swears I looked at her with scorn.

Thereafter she used me as one of the brute beasts
so roughly I ran away into the wilderness.
Which is where the angel met me and said
I was with child, that his name should be called
Ishmael, and I should return and submit to my mistress.

When my birth water broke she squatted over me
matching my every moan with made-up sounds.
She snatched my baby as he slid out,
clutched him bloody to her dry bosom.

Now she has ordered the patriarch to take me
and the boy into the desert and leave us there to die.

For she has had her womb opened in her old age
– she denied it, but she did laugh – by her own child.

She does not want her child to be brother to mine.

Abraham set us down under a thorn tree and rode away.

Ishmael's cries aimed at his heart fell short.

        The pilgrims who make Haj run between sand hills
                the way they imagined I ran frantic to find water.

I set the boy where I could not see him and prepared for us to die.

But Ishmael's cries pierced rocks and opened a well.
We found a way to live in the dry lands of Paran.
Skilled in the use of the bow my boy becomes.
He takes a wife from among the Egyptians.
Like his father the patriarch, he fathers a nation.

Be It Done Unto Me According To Your Word

So the young girl agreed
to have her temple used
for the making of the Messiah,
whom she conceives
with no help from man.

Spirit being able.

And the child grows in her
and absorbs the plain
nourishment a poor girl eats.
Her bones, her teeth, are leached
for his frame.
Her cells multiply divide and build
his flesh blood skin.

And when he was born
she examined
his infant body in hope
of seeing some evidence
of the mystery that made him.

She could detect nothing.
Then one day the child says
I must be about my father's business.

She knows what he has seen.

Soon It Is Going To Rain Milk

Run come quick
and hold out your tea mug.
A deep basin
or a tub-pan will do,

for the evening sky
is big with issue of mercy
and only the ones
(not necessarily virgins)

who have lamps full of oil
and washed vessels
are equipped to draw down
what is about to not trickle down.

This is on full.
So drink it   wash in it.
This is not
what Cleopatra bathed in
– that was mere foam
from the teats of an ass.

This is food for goodfools
who thirst and hunger
for wet that nourishes.

So stretch wide the O
of your mouth; allow
for burst of mercy clouds.

St Michael in Sitka

Dear Friend
Let us now praise the malingering postman
who did not deliver to your home address
the telegram filled with devastating news.

When I see you next we'll surely celebrate
the pock of a pothole that slowed down that
over-eager, previous, hurry-come-up hearse,

giving you a chance, when you saw it come
lumbering down live-long road to climb quick
and hide in the crownleaves of the tree of life.

We'll raise full glasses to slings and arrows
just missing their mark; and laugh uproarious
how we are blessed to have gone a bit deaf

so we no longer intercept all pointed remarks.
But mostly we will praise the big broadsword
of St Michael that he wields against mischief.

I write this to you in the town of Sitka, Alaska
where the tour guide says that Michael, who
bears resemblance to a fine-featured Ethiopian

or a head on a coin minted from dark chocolate,
arrived here in 1813 on the battleship *Neva*.
He is in full armour ablaze like a suit of light.

Our boy is clad head to toe in beaten gold.
'Beaten'. Not a word we associate with him.
Sunrays make fiery diadem round his helmet.

And though our angel looks cool and rested,
the old woman at work in the gift shop says:
All day St Michael's been flying off the shelves.

Mr Davis Runs the Voodoo Down

For fourteen minutes
and a last-lick second
Miles vacuums up
the undead
bites down, chews
then spits out.

Go on now...
leave earth!

leggo limpopo
hover hummingbird notes.

All dark of shades
all raw of silk
all run duppy blue
sole to crown
Mr Miles has arrived
to move you out
like a bailiff.
A no jestering
exorcist par excellence
jazz John the Baptist
pitching bitch at vipers
who flee from
beats to come.

For fourteen minutes
and one last-lick second,
the gorgon of horn sweeps
all duppyness clean.
Pressure drops them
five full fathoms undersea
before treading water
coming in.

Some of My Worst Wounds Again

Ah old stabs
on what plate of blood
is your knifeness
served up cold food.
Old wounds
not healed all through.
Low grade fever
from wrong done
infection.
Yes, these things come
come they will come.
Beware ones
by whom they come.

Harsh washerwoman
wicked midwife
stone throw
and hide own stink.
Need to eschew
their two-faced feasts
spread under this guise
meat of friendship
caused sharpening
of blood poison knives
flying dirty linen air
in town square.
Wash on with blood red
poison ackee foam
at the mouth bleach

washerwoman
with your dingy shift.
Scrub on and whine
striving large lady
never born to sing.
Hard on the heart and ears
these things be.
What to make of them
my poetry?

From the Bard's Book of Common Prayer

Rainy season and dry
poet clung to the side of Blue Mountains.
In solidarity with the watchman,
mothers of newborns and all working
graveyard shifts, poet forsakes sleep.

Poet leafs to petition page
in bard's book of common prayer.

Poet's Petition: Source that powers
the green shoot; good conductor of medicine
to chainey root, fever and red water grass,
since my bloom has long been delayed
clear for even me a leasehold space
fit to send down roots.

Clear for even me a leasehold space
fit to send down roots.
Clear for even me a leasehold space
fit to send down roots.
(Repeat eleven thousand times)
Till poet hears over airwaves this:

We interrupt this program to announce
that after seven and seven and seven
more lean years
a place has opened; for the poet who
sent in a request.

A space absent from Blue Mountains
in an arbor by lakes
there the young will come and feast upon
her ripeness.
Hark! cawed night bird; inner cling cling
dinged: a hint, a hint!

Miles from Kingston to Ann Arbor
the autodidact unlettered poet professes
holds doctorates in soul's musics.

Poet still keeps late vigil with so lonesome;
turns nocturnal radio to program on Mozart.
At dawn falls asleep to *Eine kleine Nachtmusik*.

The boy wonder's music enters in unforced,
seems to spring naturally as leaves to a tree (words
of other boy wonder; Keats).

Poet feasts deep. Drinks Miles Marley Mozart,
eats of sweet John Keats.

An injustice she has witnessed: the loveliest
of earth's yield laid claim to by the privileged;
this being a form of hoarding.

Medicine is Miles Marley Mozart taken in the air.
Meant to be dispensed free by the state to patients
in hospitals, schools, churches, lockups

for shut-ins to employ Miles Marley Mozart keys
to exit all places shuttered and barred.
To swing wide the stopped doors.

Sit we will on a low chair by undistressed
mahogany table. Eat exquisite meal
with some form of cornmeal; sip bellywash.

Another form of hoarding discovered in a display
on England's Romantic poets.

It says here that when they showed his visitors in
Southey snapped shut the book he was reading.
It was as if, one of them said, what was printed
therein had been set down there for his eyes alone.

Here's to the commonwealth of the written word.

Upsetter

You upsetter boy
of the beautiful eyes
last in the line
whom no one
would choose
except the keeper
of the anointing vials
friend of upstarts
and stones refused.

You youth who tore
the great she-bear
dispatcher of lions
and a giant goliath.

You came
running in
from tending
the flocks.

You chanted
as you came
the lays of a psalm
you'd composed
for the keep safe
of young animals.

Your earthly father
did not choose you.
Said there are no more
left; and he is the last
even the least.
But the prophet said
Yes, this is he.

About the Kind Who Wrestle With You All Night

Shield your eyes
the countenance of light blinds.

Held in a headlock
grab at breastfeathers.

As you reel from kidney punches
and split lip; stutter
through bloodgush;
insist:

I will not let thee go except thou bless me.

To those who sleep on stone pillow
the seraph sent to Jacob will come.
Winged boss this badboy. Mr test your mettle.

Scramble   get up   stand   after each knock down.

Accept the slight out of joint,
the drop-short rhythm
henceforth cadencing your step.
Take the one stray feather you managed
to wrench from that breast and write with it:

I did not let go until I was Blessed.

Some More Things You Do Not Know About Me

Today I stayed the day in my pink pyjamas.
Night is now about to fall and catch me with them on.

I uttered not one word.   I wrote a poem.

I brewed builders tea   deconstructed a recipe   spilled soup
on the pilot light; did a basin of hand washing,

said nothing.

Yesterday I declined to return a smile from a socialite.
I did not plastic-smile back nor swap dry biscuit remarks.

Did not kiss the air all furious.

One opportunity missed.

Nothing, alas, to be done about it.

I value my silent days. In the ground of my being
I have raised a small one-room wattle and daub hermitage.

Here I am a solitary weeper till friend Father Louis comes.
We choir   he sings lead   he was a cantor   I cant.

He'd laugh at that, rolling guffaw of a holy fool laugh.

Laugh at the one whose dime dinged a phone to screech:
'What more could you possibly want?'

And I was so in want then.

But – thanks to the Friend – what do I lack? now love brims
in my atom cups from which I drink toasts and give thanks

as I turn my thoughts to our evening dinner of rice and fish.
Rumi insists that is one way God's Love looks.

My sweetlove approaches; he unseals my mouth with kisses.

I am a Love Siren

On Irie FM at five a.m. a church sister
kickstarts an extended play

that segues seamless from hymn to hymn.

Measured in airwaves it's long as
Airdrie to Old Hope and Mountain View;

where the sister chanticleers
the great stones mother got to move.

I mother of my sweet son
who half sleeps in the next seat

cannot kick it steam engine style
like this sistren on Irie FM
who cuts and clears across
the length of Long Mountain Range;

but as we speed past Nannyville
I bid sleeping troubles, stand still.

As the sister orchestrates
removal of the great stones

I swear I see Elder Philip turning a roll.

He is trumping with exquisite Grace
along the shoulders of Long Mountain Range.
Sireen.

By Seymour Lands we passed a dread
herding a fat flock of goats
that have cropped all night on the verdant grass
in Mr Marcus Garvey's Edelweiss Park.

And now shepherd dread is leading them home
to pasture on scorch hillsides of Wareika.
Feed they will feed on dry paper and police macca

till nightfall

when they will descend again,

surefooted to graze in green pasture.

Sudden brake and dreadlocks salute:
a flash of locks then plunges the I off
into moving ranks of goat.

Oh Dread, King David was a shepherd too
tender to his father's flocks same as you;
and one day he was summoned in,
chosen over all before and anointed.

The sistren is now catching her length: sireen

Praise to unfettered spirit that bids us go
and come again

Praise to keyman compassionate

who releases from hard bondage

I go now; please Jah to come again;
watch over sweet spirit my sweet son.
Keep Jah keep him safe from harm
keep him guide spirit on the straight path
not the path of who have earned your wrath
nor of the wayward gone astray.

Keep us safe in your everlasting arms
Everlasting Mercy upon us all.
On the ones I love; on ones who love me.

To all the rest take this: love   peace.

Channelling through the Holy Ghost sistren.
Sistren who is a sireen, a love sireen.

ACKNOWLEDGEMENTS

Love and thanks to Ted, for continued nurturing and loving support. To Michael Schoenfeldt, Michael Byers, Tiya Miles, Lincoln Faller, Sid Smith, Derek Collins, Esrold Nurse, and Jane Johnson at the University of Michigan – with thanks for generous space, time, and research funding. To Dan Kelly and Hugh Wright, for the painting. To professors Eddie Baugh and Stephen Reagan, with sincere thanks. To professors Dan and Monica Chamberlin, friends, fellow travellers, and translators. To Michael Schmidt of Carcanet Press, Larry Lieberman of University of Illinois Press, Professor Jahan Ramazani of University of Virginia, and Professor Anthea Morrison of University of West Indies, Mona. To Heather Sangster, for her expert copyediting of these poems. To Ellen Seligman and Anita Chong, who are simply the best in the business.